Basic Skills

Elementary Economics

Hands-on Activities for Teaching Fundamental Economic Skills

The Toy Store & The Snack Shop for First Grade

By
Becky Daniel

Cover Design by
Matthew Van Zomeren

Inside Illustrations by
Rebecca Waske

Published by Instructional Fair • TS Denison
an imprint of

McGraw-Hill
Children's Publishing

About the Author

Becky Daniel is a parent, teacher, author, and editor. Since graduating from California University at Long Beach, she has taught kindergarten through eighth grade. She now edits *A New Day* magazine and educational books from her home in Pismo Beach, California. Over the past twenty-five years, Becky has authored more than 200 educational books for McGraw-Hill Children's Publishing and other supplemental educational publishers.

Credits

Author: Becky Daniel

Inside Illustrator: Rebecca Waske

Cover Design: Matthew Van Zomeren

Project Director/Editor: Sara Bierling

Editors: Susan Threatt, Mary Hassinger

Graphic Layout: Tracy L. Wesorick

McGraw-Hill
Children's Publishing

A Division of The McGraw·Hill Companies

Published by Instructional Fair • TS Denison
An imprint of McGraw-Hill Children's Publishing
Copyright © 2001 McGraw-Hill Children's Publishing

Send all inquiries to:
McGraw-Hill Children's Publishing
3195 Wilson Drive NW
Grand Rapids, Michigan 49544

Elementary Economics—grade 1
ISBN: 0-7424-0089-1

To the Teacher

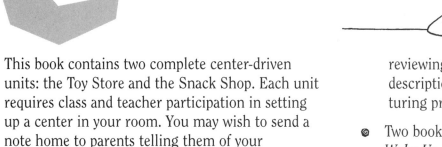

This book contains two complete center-driven units: the Toy Store and the Snack Shop. Each unit requires class and teacher participation in setting up a center in your room. You may wish to send a note home to parents telling them of your upcoming studies and asking for help in stocking your stores' shelves.

Before beginning the units, it is recommended that you introduce very basic economic principles. Explain what *money* is, where we get it, where we save it, and why we need it. Make sure students know what *goods* and *services* are and who provides them. This will naturally lead to a discussion of *producers* and *consumers*. These two words are rather lengthy for first graders, so you may want to substitute them with simpler synonyms until the students have mastered the concepts. Explain that nearly everyone is a *producer* and a *consumer*. An example of this might be a baker who has to buy (consume) flour from a producer (the mill) in order to produce (make) bread for us (the consumers) to eat. Since these units are centered on shops, you may also wish to discuss *markets* with your students. Ask them where their families shop and which stores sell which goods.

There are many children's books available for introducing and teaching economic principles. Keep several books in either your center or your classroom library. Encourage students to read as many of these books as possible. For your reference, a few books with economic themes are listed below:

◎ *Jelly Beans for Sale* by Bruce McMillan (Scholastic, 1996) presents the story of a jellybean stand staffed by two children. This book is primarily valuable for reviewing coin values, but it also includes a description of the jellybean manufacturing process.

◎ Two books that show people working are *Wake Up City!* by Alvin Tresselt (Lothrup, Lee & Shepard, 1990) and *Women Working A to Z* by Maria A. Kunstadter (Highsmith Press, 1994). It is important that your students see images of people working and connect those human resources with the positive reward of pay. Make sure they understand that you are a human resource who gets paid for producing smart students!

◎ Help students understand how things are produced with *Fire Truck Nuts and Bolts* by Jerry Boucher (Carolrhoda, 1993). Large color photographs show the step-by-step process of building a fire truck. *Extra Cheese, Please! Mozzarella's Journey from Cow to Pizza*, by Cris Peterson (Boyds Mills Press, 1994), follows the path of the milk after it leaves the cow and as it becomes mozzarella cheese that tops a family pizza. Follow the path of the grain traveling from the mill to the baker to a family in *Bread Is for Eating* by David and Phillis Gershator (Henry Holt, 1995).

During your unit of study, allow students to play in the center stores during their free time or during an indoor recess period. Many children love to play store, and this will allow them to creatively practice using money and to get comfortable with the concepts of producer and consumer. Most importantly, have fun. Economics is a big subject to comprehend, even for adults.

Table of Contents ⊚ ⊚ ⊚ ⊚ ⊚ ⊚ ⊚ ⊚ ⊚ ⊚ ⊚

Setting up Business in the Toy Store

1. Before you begin constructing your center, explain to your students that an anonymous donor (an investor) has given the class money to set up a toy store. Have students brainstorm items that should be in a toy store. Decide where you will construct the store and designate a manager (yourself). Explain to the students that the toys your store provides are goods.

2. Have students draw and color large toys, such as bikes, sleds, scooters, etc., on butcher paper. Hang the butcher paper on the back walls of the center. Make the center as colorful and inviting as possible.

3. Working from the list the students brainstormed, collect a variety of toys for the shop. Invite students to bring old toys to the classroom. Encourage them to bring toys they no longer want, so that at the end of the unit of study, an auction can take place and students can take home toys that are new to them.

4. To make the Toy Store group activities the most interesting and fun, obtain a large variety of toys. In your parent letter about the unit, mention some specific items that would be appropriate donations, such as cloth dolls, wood blocks, plastic boats, metal cars, glass marbles, paperback books, etc. Ask for toy donations from local businesses, and, if possible, buy a few new educational toys for the center.

5. Purchase play money bills. (Ideal School Supply offers American money in various denominations.) A toy cash register or money-box would be helpful but is not necessary.

6. Reproduce several copies of the Toy Store board game (pages 21–23). When the games are ready, place them on worktables in the Toy Store.

7. Reproduce several sets of the Toy Store game cards (pages 24–26). Students will use these for card games as well as the Toy Store board game. Use heavy paper or light cardboard to make the fifty-four game cards. Color code by reproducing page 23 three times and coloring red, page 24 three times and coloring blue, and page 25 three times and coloring yellow. Cut the cards apart. If cards will be used repeatedly, laminate or cover each with clear, adhesive paper.

8. Reproduce the worksheets (pages 13–18) and place them on a worktable in the Toy Store center. Students may complete these as homework assignments or for extra credit. You may also wish to complete them as a class.

9. On each day of the price setting activities (pages 6–10), each student will need his or her own copy of page 11. In preparation, choose ten different toys from the center and use adhesive colored dots to number them one through ten. Choose toys that are made of different materials, that are different sizes, fabrics, etc. Print the names of the toys on the corresponding lines of the worksheet before reproducing it for each student.

10. Culminate the unit with a toy auction. Students collect money during the unit in several ways. Give out play money for good work or allow winners of board and card games to keep their winnings. Each student should have a reclosable plastic bag marked with his or her name for holding play money.

Big Toys, Little Toys

Introduction

Each student should have his or her own copy of page 11. At the first gathering of the class in the Toy Store center, begin by discussing what resources were needed to make certain toys in the center. Then discuss the attributes of the ten numbered toys: size, color, variety of materials, quality of workmanship, etc. Show the students that each of the ten toys has a number that corresponds with a number on their worksheets. It is the objective of the first activity session to sort the ten numbered toys into sets by size: small, medium, or large. When the students are satisfied with the three piles of toys made, have them fill in the size column on their worksheets with monetary values. Small toys might be priced at $1. Medium toys might be priced at $5. Large toys might be priced at $10. The largest toy of all could be priced at $20. When everyone has finished the worksheet, hold a discussion.

Discussion Questions

1. Why do toys need to be given values?

2. What would happen if you went shopping and toys did not have price tags?

3. Do you think pricing a product by size is a good way to price it?

4. Do marbles cost less than baseball cards?

5. Do big toys usually cost more than small toys?

6. Can you name an expensive toy that is very small? An inexpensive toy that is very large?

7. Why do you think a bike usually costs more than a doll?

Follow-Up

Group students and give each group a few toys. Using the size method of placing value on toys, have the students find the total value of their toys. (Play money may be used to make these calculations.) Decide which group has the most valuable set of toys. Redistribute toys and have the groups find totals again. Total the amount of toys owned by two groups, three groups, etc. According to size, ask each student to find the total value of his or her three favorite toys in the center.

What's It Made Of?

Introduction

During the second activity session, gather the class and sort the toys in the Toy Store into sets according to the major materials used to make them, such as paper, cloth, metal, or plastic. After the toys have been sorted by material, vote as a class as to how much each kind of material should be worth. Give each category of material one of the following values: $20, $10, $5, or $1. (For example, metal and plastic toys might be worth $1, while cloth toys might be given a value of $5.) The students should determine which materials are worth more. Then hold up each of the ten numbered toys and discuss value according to the material used in making it. Have each student complete the material column on his or her worksheet with monetary values. Then hold a group discussion.

Discussion Questions

1. What do you think makes one toy more valuable than another?

2. How much do most bikes cost at a toy store? Of what are they made?

3. Why do bikes cost more than marbles?

4. If you could have any toy, what toy would you choose? What materials are needed to make your favorite toy?

Follow-Up

Divide the class into groups and assign questions from the following list to each group. (Play money should be used to find these figures. You may need to alter the questions slightly to suit the types of toys in your center.)

1. Count the number of toys made of cloth in the Toy Store center. According to the value given to cloth toys, find the total worth of all the cloth toys in the center.

2. Find out how much all the plastic toys in the center are worth when added together.

3. Figure the value of all the metal cars in the center.

4. Count the number of toys made of paper, such as playing cards. Given the value established, what is the total worth of all paper toys in the center?

5. How many different kinds of materials were used to make the toys in the center?

6. Which toy in the center was probably the most difficult to make? Why?

It's Unique and Special

Introduction

During this session, sort the toys on the pricing list into sets by their scarcity. As a group, decide how many other toys in the center are similar to each of the numbered toys. (For example, if toy #1 is a doll, count the number of dolls in the center.) Use a chalkboard to keep these tallies. When the availabilities of the toys have been determined, give the most unusual toy a value of $20. Give those that are common or readily available a value of $1. Those in the middle can be designated as $10 or $5 toys. Have students use their worksheets to complete the rare column with monetary values. When the column is complete, hold a class discussion.

Discussion Questions

1. Explain that in business, the more scarce a product, the more valuable it becomes. Which toy in the center is the most rare or unusual?

2. What are examples of scarce or rare objects around us? (antiques, one-of-a-kind, large diamonds, etc.)

3. Which do you think would cost more—a new doll or an antique doll? Why?

4. Which would most likely cost more—a doll made in your hometown or a doll made in France? Why?

5. Which is more rare, a 25-year-old baseball card or a new pair of skates? Which do you think would cost more?

6. What is the most rare toy you have at home? How did you get it? How long have you had it? Where do you keep it?

Follow-Up

Compare the most abundant set of toys with the most rare toy. Figure the value of the largest set of toys at $1 each and the value of the rarest toy at $20. Why does scarcity often make things more expensive or more popular?

Divide into groups. Have each group sort a selection of toys in several different ways:

1. oldest/newest

2. most used/rarely used

3. popular/unpopular

4. heavy/light

5. educational/recreational

Take Your Pick

Introduction

In this session, determine the popularity of certain toys by having students choose their favorites. Line up the ten numbered toys on the pricing list in order of preference. Have each student complete the popular column on his or her worksheet by giving his or her most favorite toy a value of $20, the least favorite toy a value of $1, and toys in the middle a value of $10 or $5. Follow with a group discussion.

Discussion Questions

1. What makes some toys more popular than others?

2. Which of the toys were chosen as favorites most often by classmates?

3. What do the toys chosen as class favorites have in common with each other?

4. Did you choose a rare toy as your favorite?

5. If you were choosing your favorite toy a year ago, would it have been the same as you chose today? Three years ago?

6. In five years, with which of the toys do you think you still might enjoy playing?

7. Are your favorite toys (the ones you rated $20 or $10) made of the same materials?

Follow-Up

In small groups, have the students sort a selection of toys according to popularity. How many in the group chose a particular toy as a favorite? Which toy in the center was chosen most often as a favorite? As a group, vote to choose the most popular toy in the center. Make a graph to show how popular each toy is with the class.

The Price Setting Sessions

Introduction

After determining sets of toys based on size, material, rarity, and popularity, culminate with a session comparing the four ways of placing value on each toy. Each student needs his or her completed worksheet for this session. Using play money, have students find a total price by combining all four values for each of the ten numbered toys. (These totals will vary with individuals, given the popularity category.) When a total value has been put on all ten toys, have the students take turns arranging the toys in a parade with the most valuable toy in front, followed by second most valuable, etc. Hold a class discussion comparing the different rankings.

Discussion Questions

1. Are the four prices given for each toy consistent? How do they vary?

2. Which attributes—size, material, rarity, or popularity—seem to be most similar?

3. Which attribute—size, material, rarity, or popularity—do you think is the most important to consider when pricing a toy?

4. Why do you think the toy most often valued the highest was so popular with classmates?

5. Why do you think something popular is more valuable than something unpopular?

6. Which of the four attributes—size, material, rarity, or popularity—do you think places the most accurate value on toys?

Follow-Up

Using play money and looking at the completed worksheets, have students count out the bills needed to pay all four values for a select few of the toys listed.

Name_____

	Size	Material	Rare	Popular	Total
1.					
2.					
3.					
4.					
5.					
6.					
7.					
8.					
9.					
10.					

  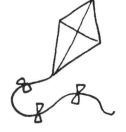

Shopping for Toys

Try to arrange a visit to a toy store that carries a wide variety of toys. Before you go, discuss what students might see. Give the students specific things to look for and questions to ask the toy store clerk. When you get back to the classroom, discuss the questions and compare answers.

Sample Questions:

1. What is the most expensive toy in the store?

2. What is the most rare toy in the store?

3. Which toys are most often purchased?

4. Which are the most inexpensive toys?

5. Which are the biggest toys?

6. What is your favorite toy in the store?

7. What is your least favorite toy in the store?

8. If you could make toys, what kind would you make? Why?

9. Why does the toy store clerk work in the store?

The Great Toy Auction

Getting Ready

During the Toy Store unit of study, award good work with play money. Also use play money as prizes for winning card and board games. Then auction off the toys in the center using the money earned during the study unit.

Rules

Holding up one toy at a time, students raise one hand to indicate a bid. (Everyone should have help counting his or her money before the auction so they will know their limit for bidding. You may wish to discuss budgets with the students at this time.)

Illustrating Choices

Draw a picture of a toy that best fits in each category.

Expensive	Rare	Cheap
Popular	**Hard to Make**	**Heavy**
Strong	**Soft**	**Collectible**

Wants and Needs

Name_____

Circle each need. Draw an **X** on each want.

Sorting It All Out

Name_____

Use the color code to color the toys according to the materials used to make them. If the toy is made of a combination of materials, color it all colors necessary (for example, a jump rope might have a purple rope and brown handles).

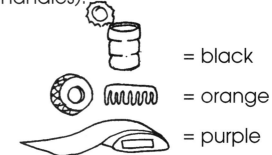

= brown

= green

= yellow

= black

= orange

= purple

The Price Is Right

Name_____

Color the bills to show the price of each toy.

 $16.00 $10.00

 $4.00

$2.00    $5.00 $3.00

1.

$1	$1
	$1
	$5
	$10

2.

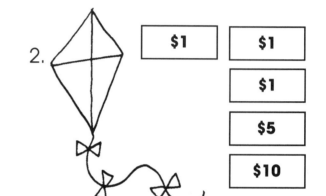

$1	$1
	$1
	$5
	$10

3.

$1	$1
	$1
	$5

4.

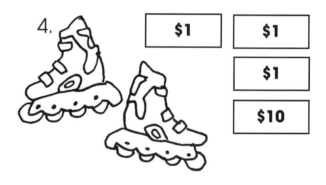

$1	$1
	$1
	$10

5.

$1	$1
$1	$1
	$1
	$5

6.

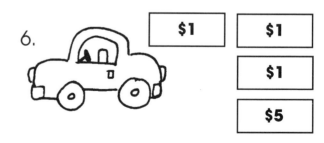

$1	$1
	$1
	$5

Which Costs More?

Use play money to help you find the cost of the toys. Circle the toy in each line that costs more.

 $16.00 $10.00  $4.00

$2.00 $5.00 $3.00

1.

2.

3.

4.

5.

6.

Change Please

Name_____

Use play money to find out how much change you would get when buying toys. Color in the correct amount of money.

 $16.00    $10.00 $4.00

 $2.00 $5.00 $3.00

Buy	**Pay**	**Change**				
1. 	$20.00	$1	$1	$1	$1	$1
2. 	$10.00	$1	$1	$1	$1	$1
3.	$5.00	$1	$1	$1	$1	$1
4. 	$10.00	$1	$1	$1	$1	$1
5.	$5.00	$1	$1	$1	$1	$1
6. 	$5.00	$1	$1	$1	$1	$1

IF5180 *Elementary Economics*

Toy Store Rummy

Players: 2 to 4

Object of the Game: to get rummies and collect play money for the toy auction

Rules:

1. Shuffle one set of Toy Store game cards.

2. Deal each player seven cards.

3. Stack the rest of the cards facedown on the table between the players. Turn the top card faceup in a discard pile.

4. Place play money on the table for the bank.

5. Moving clockwise, players take turns drawing and discarding one card in an attempt to collect three of the same toys that are the same color or one of each color. When a player has three of the same kind of toy in the same color or one in each color, he or she makes a "fan" and places those three cards down.

6. When a player has a second fan of three of a kind, he or she places them down, discards the seventh card, and yells, "Rummy."

7. Each time a player gets Rummy, he or she collects $10.00 from the bank. Players save the play money they win for use at the toy auction.

Toy Crazy
◉ ◉ ◉ ◉ ◉ ◉ ◉

Players: 2 to 4

Object of the Game: to collect money for the toy auction

Rules:

1. Give each player $74.00 in play money. Shuffle one set of Toy Store game cards and deal five to each player. The rest of the deck is placed facedown in the center of the table. This is the draw pile. The top card is turned faceup next to the draw pile.

2. Each player takes a turn matching the top card on the discard pile by color or kind of toy.

3. Bicycles are wild cards and can be played on any toy or color card. The color of the bicycle card played is the new color to match.

4. If a player cannot match the top card with a card in his or her hand, he or she draws another card. If he or she still cannot play, the turn passes to the next player.

5. When one player has gone out by discarding all cards, he or she is declared the winner of the round. Each player pays the winner $5.00 in play money. Players keep their money for the toy auction.

Toy Store War
◉ ◉ ◉ ◉ ◉ ◉ ◉ ◉ ◉ ◉

Players: 2 to 4

Object of the Game: to collect play money for the toy auction

Rules:

1. Shuffle one set of Toy Store game cards and deal them all out. (If there are two players, each will have twenty-seven cards; three players will each have eighteen cards; or four players will each have thirteen cards, with two discarded.) Players place their piles of cards facedown.

2. Players take turns turning over their top two cards. The player with the highest total value of toys showing takes all the face-up cards. (Play money can be used to figure and compare the totals.) If there is a tie for highest value of cards showing, everyone keeps his or her own cards.

3. When everyone has gone through his or her stack of face-down cards, each player counts his or her cards. Players award the player with the most cards $5.00 of their play money. Repeat the game until time is called.

The Toy Store

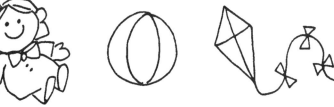

⊚ ⊚ ⊚ ⊚ ⊚ ⊚ ⊚ ⊚ ⊚ ⊚

Players: 2 to 4

Getting Ready to Play: This game is played like Monopoly®. The object is to buy toys wholesale, sell them retail, and eventually to collect monopolies of toys.

1. Reproduce the game board on pages 22 and 23. Attach it to the inside of a file folder. Cut out the Toy Store rules and paste them to the front of the file folder game board. Use markers to decorate it, then laminate for durability.

2. Gather the game board you made and one set of Toy Store game cards (fifty-four cards).

3. Sort the six kinds of toy cards (kite, doll, ball, skates, car, bicycle) and place all nine bicycle cards in a stack, all nine car cards in a stack, etc.

4. To play this game, participants need a pair of dice, play money bills, and from two to four game markers depending on the number of players.

Toy Store Rules ⊚

1. Each player receives $74.00 (two $20s, two $10s, two $5s, and four $1s).

2. All players place their markers in the space marked GO. Roll the dice to see who goes first.

3. The first player rolls the dice and moves the indicated number of spaces. When a player lands on a particular toy, if those toys have not been bought by another player, he or she may buy all nine of the toy cards for $10.00. If he or she buys those cards, then that player is in the business of selling that particular kind of toy. A player does not have to buy a toy business while on a particular space unless he or she chooses.

4. Players continue rolling the dice and moving around the board. Each time a player passes GO, he or she collects $20.00.

5. If a player lands on a toy space owned by another player, he or she can pay in two ways: give one of that particular toy card back (if previously purchased) or pay the amount shown on the toy card and receive a card. If a player does not have a card or enough money to pay the toy dealer, he or she must drop out of the game. If a toy retailer runs out of a particular toy card, he or she is no longer in the business of selling that toy, and no one pays when landing on that space.

6. Play continues until one player has accumulated all of the money, or time is called. If time is called, players add up their assets ($1.00 per toy card), plus cash, to determine the winner. Students should keep their cash to use at the toy auction.

The Toy Store

GO Collect $20

IF5180 *Elementary Economics*

$16

$10

$5

$4

$3

$2

$16

$10

$5

$4

$3

$2

IF5180 *Elementary Economics*

$16

$10

$5

$4

$3

$2

The Snack Shop Center Set-Up

Construct a Snack Shop center in your classroom using a combination of real snacks and empty packages. Include play money, activity sheets, and games, so students may buy and sell snacks to each other in free play. Gather in the center as a class to participate in the structured games, activities, and worksheets that follow.

1. Before constructing your center, ask students where they buy snacks. Find out what snacks they buy, who sells them, and who pays for them. Then explain that you will be setting up a snack shop. Have students brainstorm a list of items to be sold in the snack shop. Designate one student as manager who will copy your list of snacks from the chalkboard.

2. Designate one area of your classroom as the Snack Shop. On a large piece of butcher paper, have students draw and color or paint shelves and carts full of snacks. Hang the butcher paper on the back walls of the center. Make the center as colorful and inviting as possible. Small baskets with handles that can be used to sort and display the snacks should be placed in the center.

3. Collect snack containers for the center. Invite students to bring in empty snack containers for the center. Line up containers in baskets on bookcase shelves, tables, etc. To make the Snack Shop group activities (pages 28–31) the most interesting and fun, obtain a large variety of snack food containers. Include peanut cans, pretzel bags, candy boxes, cookie tins, etc.

4. Purchase play money coins. (Ideal School Supply offers American money in various denominations.) A toy cash register or moneybox would be helpful but is not necessary.

5. Reproduce several copies of the Snack Shop board game (pages 42–44). When completed, place the games on worktables in the center.

6. Reproduce several sets of the Snack Shop game cards (pages 45–47). Use heavy paper or light cardboard to make the thirty-six game cards. Color the snacks on the cards as follows: pretzels—red; peanuts—orange; cookies—yellow; chips and raisins—purple. Cut the cards apart. If cards will be used repeatedly, laminate or cover each with clear, adhesive paper.

7. Reproduce the worksheets (pages 32–38) and place them on a worktable in the center. Assign these as class- or homework or use them as a group to supplement a center session.

8. Give each student a reclosable plastic bag for keeping play coins. Explain that at the end of the unit there will be a snack shop picnic, and each student will buy his or her food with play coins earned during the unit of study. This will give you an opportunity to discuss budgets.

The Long and Short of It

The activities on this page and those on pages 29 and 30 have been especially designed to be completed using real snacks. Each day's activity involves a different snack—cookies, pretzels, or nuts. Using a variety of snacks, you will be able to show the students how value is placed on products by size, scarcity, quality, and popularity. Be sure to record the original price of each package of snacks for comparison.

Introduction

At the introduction of the Snack Shop unit and center, you will need bags of cookies. Try to find cookies that vary in size from very small to quite large, for example, rectangular cookies like graham crackers, round ones like chocolate chip cookies, and square ones like wafers. Begin by discussing that snacks come in all sizes and aren't usually sold for a special price per item, but are sold by weight. Have the students estimate the number of cookies in each purchased container. Count the cookies in each container to see which student came closest to the actual number. You may want to create a graph to compare the number of cookies in each bag. Are there more small cookies in a bag than large cookies, more round cookies in a bag than square cookies? Give each student a small, medium, and large cookie. Have the students measure their three cookies with rulers. Hold a discussion to consider the different ways cookies are priced.

Discussion Questions

1. Show two different bags of cookies—a small bag with just a few cookies and a large bag with a lot of cookies. Ask, "Would it be fair to sell all bags of cookies for the same price? Why or why not?"

2. Holding up a very large cookie and a small one, compare individual cookies and ask, "If all cookies are sold for 25¢ each, would that be fair? Would you pay 25¢ for a big cookie or for a small cookie?"

3. Read the weight on two bags of cookies. Count the cookies in the bags and compare with the weight. Ask, "Would it be fair if all cookies were sold by the pound (kg)?"

4. Which seems more economical (logical)—selling cookies by the bag, by individual cookie, or by weight? Why?

Follow-Up

Cut one of each kind of cookie in half. Have the students try to name the ingredients in each as you list them on the chalkboard. Then read the ingredients on each bag of cookies. Compare with the answers the students gave. Why do some cookies cost more than others? Do chocolate chip cookies cost more to make than plain sugar cookies. Why or why not? Do peanut butter cookies cost more than gingersnaps? Compare prices of different cookies.

The Big Pretzel Day

Introduction

For another look at a method of placing value on snacks, you will need a variety of pretzels. Try to buy as many varieties of pretzels (shapes, sizes, flavors) as you can find in your local supermarket—at least six different kinds. You may also wish to send a letter to parents asking for donations. When you buy the pretzels, make a note of the different prices for each bag or box. Buy big pretzel sticks, little pretzel sticks, pretzel snacks with fillings, and flavored pretzels.

Place each kind of pretzel in a separate bowl. Have students taste each kind of pretzel and give a rating of excellent (3 points), good (2 points), or okay (1 point). Keep track of this rating by listing all the snack varieties on the chalkboard and having students line up and taste each kind of snack as you record the ratings. When all of the pretzels have been tasted, add up the points to see which pretzels were the favorites. Follow with a discussion.

Discussion Questions

1. Do you think all pretzels taste the same?

2. What qualities contribute to a good pretzel?

3. Do all bags of pretzels cost the same? Are all bags of pretzels the same size? Do all bags contain the same number of pretzels?

4. Of what are pretzels made?

5. Why do you think some pretzels cost more than others?

6. Have you ever tasted a soft pretzel? How much do you think most large, soft pretzels cost?

7. How much would you pay for a pretzel? (10¢, 25¢, 50¢?) What is the most you would pay for a pretzel?

Follow-Up

Compare the prices of the pretzels that you bought with the students' ratings. Did the pretzels they like best cost the most? Why or why not? On the chalkboard, make a list of reasons that the students think some pretzels are more expensive than others?

It's Nutty!

Introduction

In the third Snack Shop session, you will need a variety of nuts. Some common varieties are peanuts, macadamia nuts, walnuts, almonds, pecans, and hazelnuts. (Be conscious of any allergies students in your class may have.) Talk about how certain nuts are grown in certain climates. Macadamia nuts are tropical and grow in Hawaii. Peanuts grow in warm climates like Africa. Look at a map and find the places where peanuts are grown. Examples are Georgia, India, China, Nigeria, and Indonesia. Which peanut-producing location is closest to where your school is located? Which peanut-producing location is the farthest from your school? Examine the price on each container of nuts.

Discussion Questions

1. Where are peanuts grown? Where are macadamia nuts grown? Which cost more?

2. How do you think nuts get from where they are grown to the market?

3. If a peanut were grown in your neighborhood, would it cost less than a peanut grown in Africa and shipped to your neighborhood? What factors contribute to the cost?

4. What are some nuts grown in your area? (This is an opportunity to discuss specialization. If you're good at something, you produce only that.)

5. What are some nuts not grown in your area? Do they cost more in the supermarket?

Follow-Up

Play a relay game. Divide the students into three teams. Give each team a bag of peanuts. Assign a different place each team is to distribute its peanuts to one at a time. For example, one team places peanuts near the playground fence. One places peanuts under a basketball hoop. One places them just outside the classroom door. Race to see which relay team can carry its peanuts the fastest, one at a time, to its team's destination. When one team has distributed all of its peanuts, call time. Discuss why some teams were able to deliver more peanuts.

End the session by looking at a variety of distances on a map.

- Show how far African peanuts have to be shipped to Alaska.
- Show how far Hawaiian macadamia nuts have to be shipped to England.

Snack Shop Shopping

Arrange for students to visit a snack shop or a supermarket snack display. Meet with a store manager and have students find out the following:

1. What is the most expensive snack sold at the store?

2. What is the least expensive snack sold at the store?

3. Which snack travels the longest distance?

4. Which snack is the most difficult to keep fresh (perishable)?

5. What happens to snacks that are too old to sell?

6. Approximately how many packages of cookies does the store sell per day?

7. Approximately how many containers of nuts does the store sell per day?

8. What is the most popular pretzel the store sells?

9. What is the most popular cookie sold at the store?

10. What is the most popular nut sold at the store?

11. What is the most popular snack sold at the store?

12. Which kinds of snacks are usually sold in boxes, cans, or bags?

Snack Treat Picnic

Have each student bring a container of his or her favorite snack to class—enough to share. Discuss inflation and how having lots of money drives up prices. Have students count their money. Check to see how much money the average student has. If the average student has $200 worth of coins, the snacks will need to be expensive. After a discussion, give each snack a value (small pretzel sticks could be 5¢ each, peanuts could be 20¢ a cup, etc.) Then place small portions of the snacks in paper cups or on napkins. Students use the play money they have collected during the unit to buy the treats.

Goods and Services

Name_____

Look at the pictures. If the worker provides a good, write a **G** on the line. If the worker provides a service, write an **S** on the line.

Wrapping It Up

In each of the containers—can, bag, box, and jar—draw at least three different kinds of snacks that are sold in that type of container.

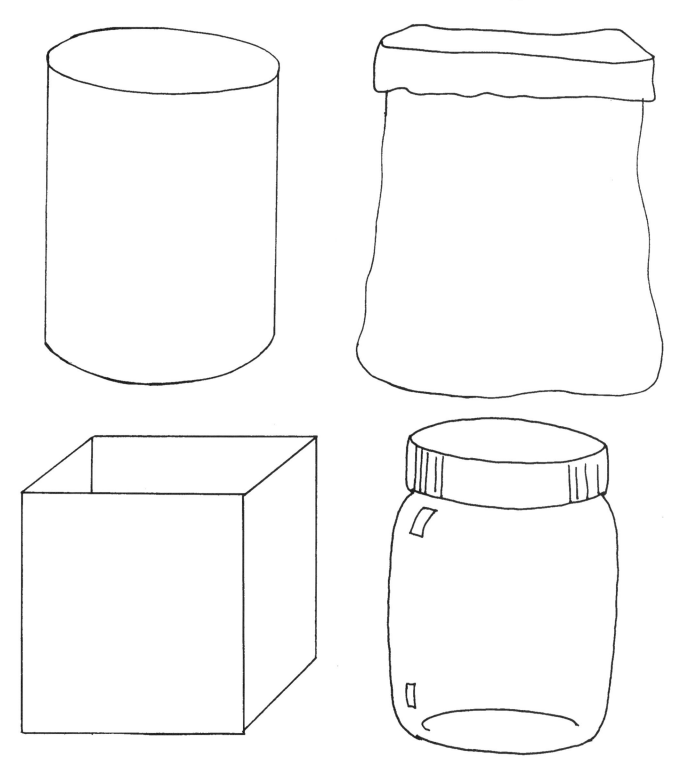

Designing a Wrapper

Name_____

Attractive wrappers help sell snacks. Imagine you are an artist for a large snack manufacturer. Design a box for your favorite snack food.

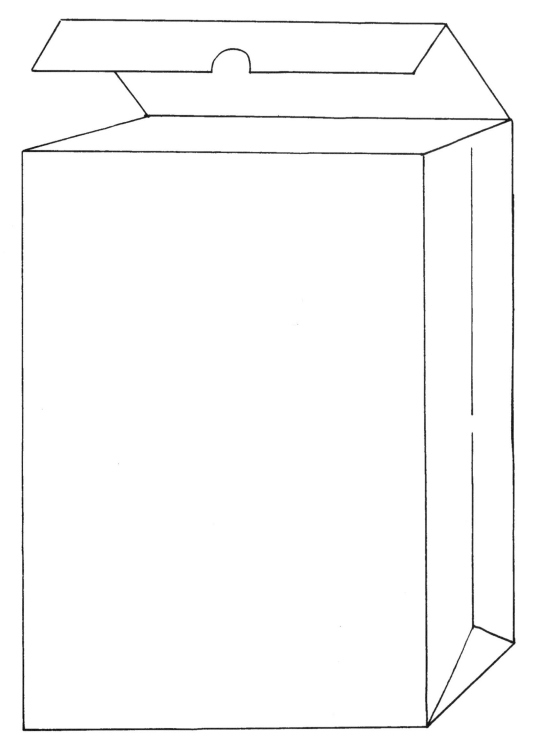

Which Is More?

Name_____

 5¢   10¢   15¢

 25¢   50¢

Using paper coins, find the cost of each snack. Circle the one in each line that is more expensive.

1.

2.

3.

4.

5.

6.

7.

8.

IF5180 *Elementary Economics*

Bagging a Snack

Name_____

 5¢   10¢    15¢

 25¢   50¢

Draw snacks in each bag that total the amount shown. You may use paper coins to help you figure the amounts.

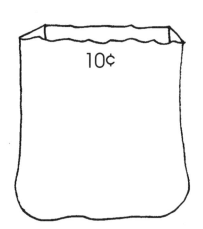
10¢

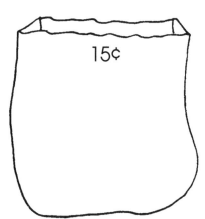
15¢

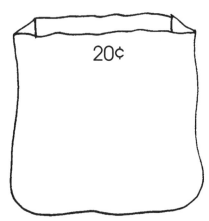
20¢

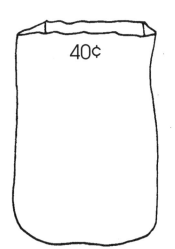
40¢

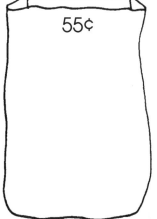
55¢

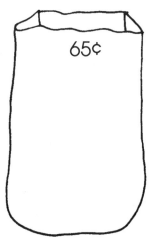
65¢

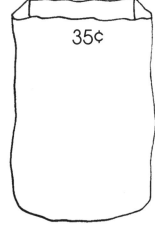
35¢

 IF5180 *Elementary Economics*

Buying Snacks

Name_____

 5¢   10¢   15¢

 25¢   50¢

Color the coins needed to buy each snack.

1. = 5¢ 10¢ 25¢ 50¢

2. = 5¢ 10¢ 25¢ 50¢

3. = 5¢ 10¢ 25¢ 50¢

4. = 5¢ 10¢ 25¢ 50¢

5. = 5¢ 10¢ 25¢ 50¢

6. = 5¢ 10¢ 25¢ 50¢

7. = 5¢ 10¢ 25¢ 50¢

8. = 5¢ 10¢ 25¢ 50¢

Favorite Snacks

Name_____

Color the snacks.

Snacks I love = red
Snacks I like = blue
Snacks I don't like = yellow

1. How much would it cost to buy all the snacks you love?

_____

2. How much would it cost to buy all the snacks you like?

_____

3. How much would it cost to buy all the snacks you don't like?

_____

4. How much would it cost to buy all the snacks?

_____

⊚ne D⊚llar Rummy

Players: 2 to 4

Object of the Game: to collect a set of cards with a value of exactly $1.00

Rules:

1. This game is played in several rounds.

2. Shuffle one set of Snack Shop game cards and deal each player six.

3. Stack the rest of the cards facedown on the table between the players, with the top card faceup.

4. Moving clockwise, players take turns drawing and discarding one card at a time in an attempt to collect a set of cards with an exact value of $1.00. A player may take a discarded card that is faceup or the top card that is facedown. When a player has a set of cards (may be two, three, or more) with a total value of $1.00, he or she makes a "fan" and lays those cards down. That player then gets another turn.

5. If all the facedown cards have been played, shuffle the discard pile and place them facedown, turning over the top card.

6. Play continues until one player has put all of his or her cards down. Then each player collects the amount of coins represented by the snack cards he or she has been able to play. For example, a player with one fan of snack cards will get $1.00; a player with two fans will receive $2.00. Cards held in a player's hand do not count for or against him or her.

7. Shuffle the cards and deal again. After every round of play, players keep their coins for buying real snacks during the Snack Treat Picnic (see page 31).

Go Get Snacks

Players: 2 to 4

Object of the Game: to collect three sets of identical cards

Rules:

1. Shuffle one set of Snack Shop game cards and deal each player six.

2. Stack the rest of the cards facedown, except the top card, which is placed faceup. If players have any exact matches, they lay them down.

3. Moving clockwise, players take turns asking each other for cards. "Do you have three pretzels?" If the person asked has that card, he or she gives it to the player who can then make a match. That person gets another turn. If the player asked does not have a card, he or she responds, "Go get snacks." The player then must draw one card from the top of the deck or pick up the face-up card and discard one.

4. Players continue asking for cards or drawing and discarding in an attempt to collect three pairs. When one player has collected three pairs, everyone totals the amount of the cards that he or she has placed down and receives that amount of paper coins. All players keep their coins for buying real snacks during the Snack Treat Picnic (see page 31).

Colorful Snacks

Players: 2 to 4

Object of the Game: to collect six cards that are the same color

Rules:

1. Shuffle one set of Snack Shop game cards and deal each player six.

2. Stack the rest of the cards facedown, except the top card, which is placed faceup.

3. Moving clockwise, players take turns drawing one card (or taking the faceup card) and discarding one card in an attempt to get six of the same color.

4. When a player has six of the same color, he or she is declared the winner and receives paper coins totaling the face value of his or her six cards. Players keep all the coins they receive for the Snack Treat Picnic (see page 31).

Go Fish for Snacks

Players: 2 to 4

Object of the Game: to practice using coins to buy snack cards

Rules:

1. Shuffle one set of Snack Shop game cards and deal each player seven.

2. Stack the rest of the cards facedown, except the top card, which is placed faceup. Place play coins on the table for a bank.

3. Moving clockwise, players take turns drawing and discarding one card in an attempt to collect matching snacks. When a player has two of a kind, he or she may sell them to the bank and collect the appropriate paper coins. For example, a pair might be a 2 peanuts card and a 3 peanuts card worth a total of 50¢. (The numbers on the cards do not have to match, just the kind of snack.)

4. When one player has sold three sets of matching snacks and drawn a match for his or her seventh card, he or she collects the money for the last pair, and the round of play is over. Players keep their money to spend at the Snack Treat Picnic (see page 31).

The Snack Shop

Players: 2 to 4

Getting Ready to Play: The object of the game is to buy the most snack cards.

1. Reproduce the game board found on pages 43 and 44. Attach it to the inside of a file folder. Cut out the Snack Shop rules and attach them to the front of the file folder. Use markers to decorate it, then laminate for durability.

2. Gather one set of Snack Shop game cards (thirty-six cards) and $4.00 worth of play coins for each player, plus extra money for the bank. To play this game, participants need a pair of dice and from two to four game markers.

Snack Shop Rules

1. Each player is to receive $4.00 in play coins (5 nickels, 5 dimes, 5 quarters, and 4 half-dollars). Place more coins in the center of the game board for making change.

2. Tuck the edge of matching cards faceup around the edge of the game board next to the same snack space. (For example, two cards with one box of raisins each are placed on the edge of the board next to the space showing one box of raisins.) Players will easily be able to see which snacks are for sale.

3. Each person places his or her marker on the GO space. Roll the dice to see who has the highest total. That person has the first turn.

4. The first player rolls the dice and moves clockwise the number of spaces indicated by the dice. The player has the option of buying a snack card when he or she lands on a snack space.

5. Each player who rolls doubles gets an extra turn. Each time a player passes GO, he or she collects 50¢ from the bank.

6. Players continue taking turns, rolling the dice, and moving around the board. Each time a player lands on a snack card space, he or she may buy one of the cards. When both the cards from a space have been purchased, and a player lands on that space, he or she cannot buy a snack.

7. When one player runs out of money, time is called. Players cannot run out of money without paying the exact amount they have left to buy a snack. For example, if a player has 50¢ left, he or she can buy a card with a box of raisins or a card with two bags of chips. Play continues until one player is out of money, all the snack cards have been collected, or time is called. At the end of the game, each player totals the amount of snacks he or she has purchased. The player with the most value in snacks is declared the winner.

The Snack Shop

5 cookies
15¢ each
75¢

5 pretzels
5¢ each
25¢

2 bags of peanuts
10¢ each
20¢

1 bag of chips
25¢ each
25¢

4 cookies
15¢ each
60¢

4 pretzels
5¢ each
20¢

1 cookie
15¢ each
15¢

10¢
2 pretzels   5¢ each

40¢
4 bags of peanuts
10¢ each

50¢
1 box of raisins
50¢ each

30¢
3 bags of peanuts
10¢ each

The Snack Shop

3 cookies   15¢ each
45¢

2 pretzels   5¢ each
10¢

5 bags of peanuts   10¢ each
50¢

1 pretzel   5¢ each
5¢

3 cookies   15¢ each
45¢

2 bags of chips   25¢ each
50¢

1 bag of peanuts   10¢ each
10¢

15¢   3 pretzels   5¢ each

30¢   2 cookies   15¢ each

20¢   2 bags of peanuts   10¢ each

GO

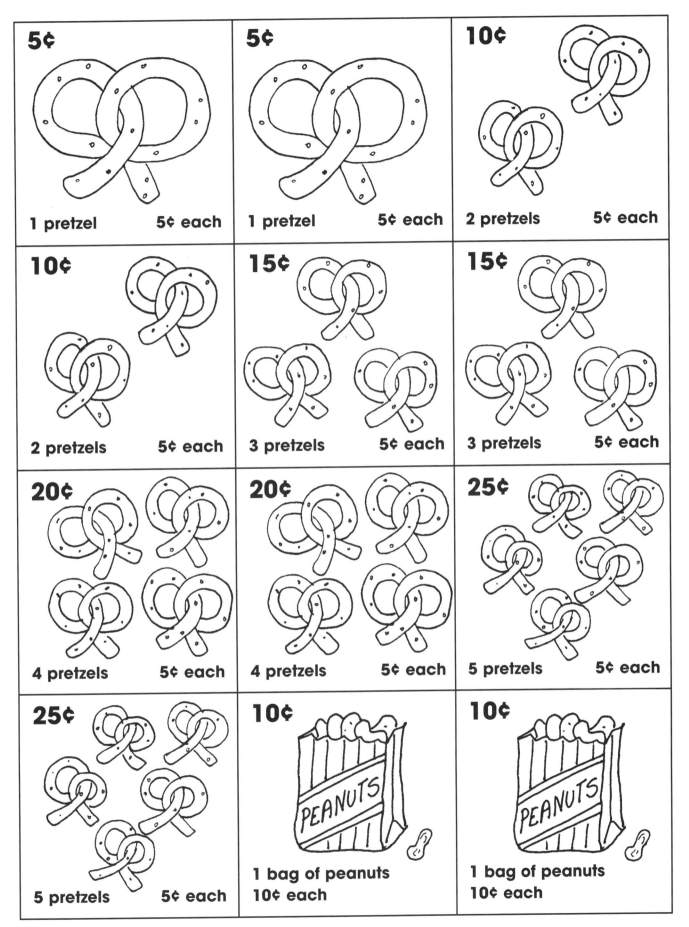

5¢

1 pretzel   5¢ each

5¢

1 pretzel   5¢ each

10¢

2 pretzels   5¢ each

10¢

2 pretzels   5¢ each

15¢

3 pretzels   5¢ each

15¢

3 pretzels   5¢ each

20¢

4 pretzels   5¢ each

20¢

4 pretzels   5¢ each

25¢

5 pretzels   5¢ each

25¢

5 pretzels   5¢ each

10¢

1 bag of peanuts
10¢ each

10¢

1 bag of peanuts
10¢ each

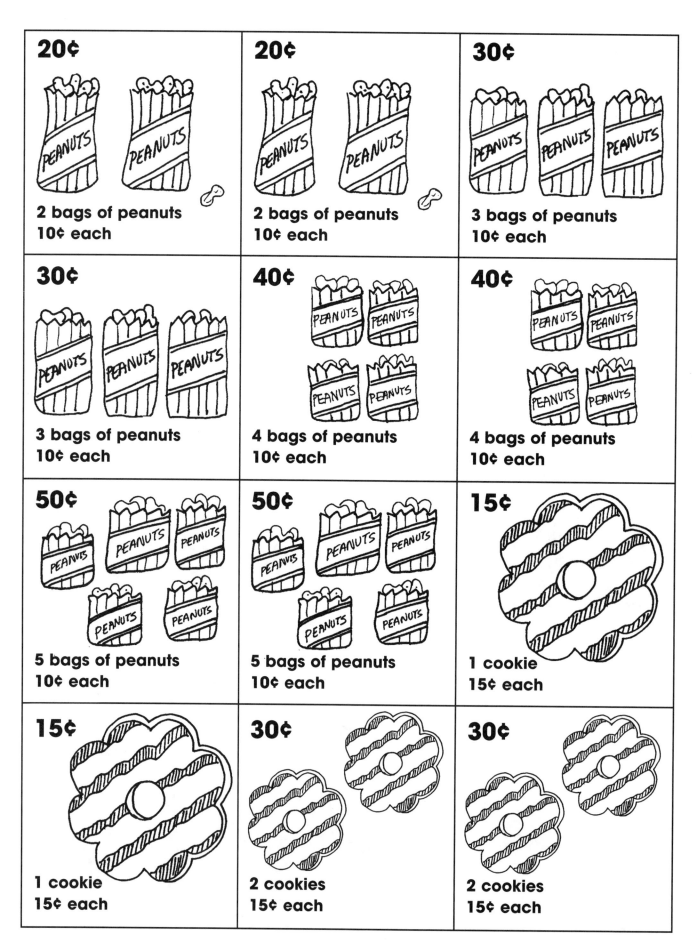

20¢

2 bags of peanuts
10¢ each

20¢

2 bags of peanuts
10¢ each

30¢

3 bags of peanuts
10¢ each

30¢

3 bags of peanuts
10¢ each

40¢

4 bags of peanuts
10¢ each

40¢

4 bags of peanuts
10¢ each

50¢

5 bags of peanuts
10¢ each

50¢

5 bags of peanuts
10¢ each

15¢

1 cookie
15¢ each

15¢

1 cookie
15¢ each

30¢

2 cookies
15¢ each

30¢

2 cookies
15¢ each

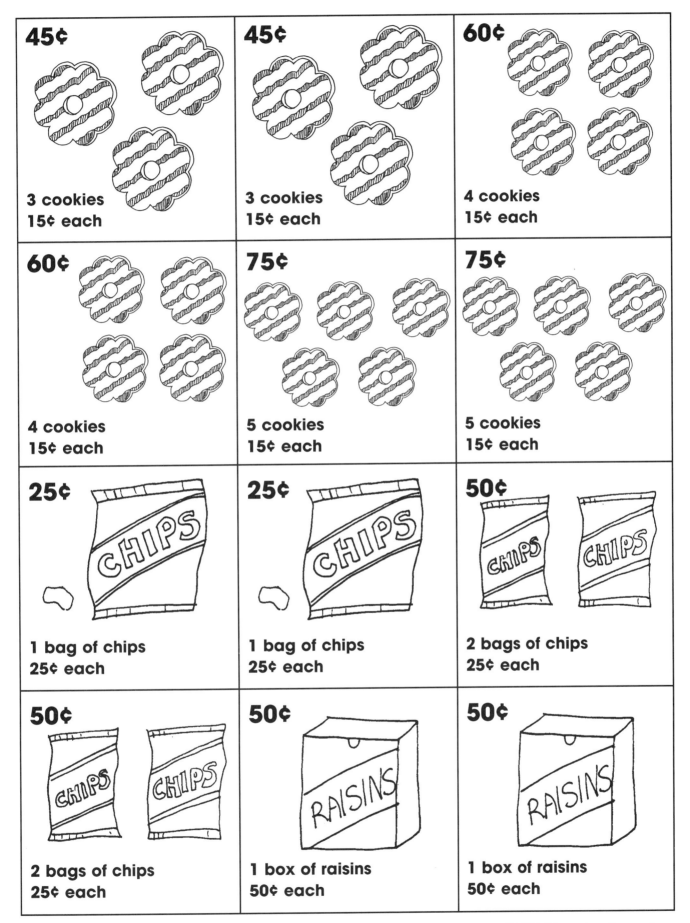

45¢

3 cookies
15¢ each

45¢

3 cookies
15¢ each

60¢

4 cookies
15¢ each

60¢

4 cookies
15¢ each

75¢

5 cookies
15¢ each

75¢

5 cookies
15¢ each

25¢

1 bag of chips
25¢ each

25¢

1 bag of chips
25¢ each

50¢

2 bags of chips
25¢ each

50¢

2 bags of chips
25¢ each

50¢

1 box of raisins
50¢ each

50¢

1 box of raisins
50¢ each

Answer Key

Illustrating Choices 13
Answers will vary.

Wants and Needs 14
Needs: fruit, meal, house, hug, clothes
Wants: bike, kite, ball, in-line skates, teddy bear, toy plane, comics

Sorting It All Out 15
toy plane—black, orange
jump rope—brown, purple
comics—green
kite—brown, purple, green
toy car—black, orange
in-line skates—black, orange
stuffed bear—orange, purple
binoculars—yellow, black, orange
doll—orange, purple

The Price Is Right 16
1. 1 one-dollar bill, 1 five-dollar bill, and 1 ten-dollar bill
2. 2 one-dollar bills
3. 3 one-dollar bills
4. 1 ten-dollar bill
5. 4 one-dollar bills
6. 1 five-dollar bill

Which Costs More? 17
1. bike
2. doll
3. ball
4. doll
5. car
6. car

Change Please 18
1. 4 bills
2. 0 bills
3. 1 bill
4. 5 bills
5. 2 bills
6. 3 bills

Goods and Services 32
G: toy maker, fisherman, snack shop clerk, cook, shoe salesperson
S: school bus driver, firefighter, vet, plumber

Wrapping It Up 33
Answers will vary.

Designing a Wrapper 34
Answers will vary.

Which Is More? 35
1. peanuts
2. raisins
3. cookie
4. cookie
5. raisins
6. cookie
7. raisins
8. chips

Bagging a Snack 36
Answers will vary.

Buying Snacks 37
1. 1 nickel
2. 1 nickel, 1 dime
3. 1 dime
4. 1 quarter
5. 1 half-dollar
6. 1 half-dollar
7. 1 nickel, 1 quarter
8. 1 nickel, 1 dime

Favorite Snacks 38
Most answers will vary.
4. $1.05

IF5180 *Elementary Economics*